cooking the Indian way

Stuffed with either meat or vegetable filling, *samosas* make a tasty snack or light lunch. (Recipe on page 20.)

cooking the Indian way

VIJAY MADAVAN

PHOTOGRAPHS BY ROBERT L. & DIANE WOLFE

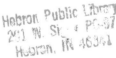

easy menu
ethnic
cookbooks

Lerner Publications Company ▪ Minneapolis

Drawings and Map by Jeanette Swofford
Photographs on pages 12, 14, and 20 by Judy Frater

The page border for this book is based on the wheel that is
found on the Indian flag. It is an ancient Indian symbol that
stands for the powers and changes of nature.

To my husband, Steve

Copyright © 1985 by Lerner Publications Company

Library of Congress Cataloging in Publication Data

Madavan, Vijay.
    Cooking the Indian way.

    (Easy menu ethnic cookbooks)
    Includes index.
    Summary: An introduction to the cooking of India
featuring such traditional recipes as lamb kebabs,
yogurt chicken, pumpkin curry, and apple chutney.
Also includes information on the geography, customs,
people of India.
    1. Cookery, Indic—Juvenile literature. [1. Cookery,
Indic] I. Wolfe, Robert L., ill. II. Wolfe, Diane,
ill. III. Title. IV. Series.
TX724.5.I4M26   1985   641.5954   84-28906
ISBN 0-8225-0911-3 (lib. bdg.)

Manufactured in the United States of America

5 6 7 8 9 10 – P/JR – 98 97 96 95 94 93

**Ground lamb kebabs taste especially good when
eaten with apple chutney. (Recipes on pages 25
and 43.)**

CONTENTS

INTRODUCTION, 7
 The People of India, 7
 The Varied Traditions of Indian Food, 8
 Spices: Sweet, Hot, Savory, 11
 A Passage to India, 11

BEFORE YOU BEGIN, 12
 Special Ingredients, 12
 Cooking Utensils, 14
 Cooking Terms, 15
 Preparing Indian Foods, 16
 Indian Meals, 16

AN INDIAN MENU, 18

MEAT AND FISH DISHES, 20
 Deep-Fried Stuffed Savory Pastries, 20
 Spiced Ground Meat, 23
 Garam Masala, 24
 Ground Lamb Kebabs, 25
 Yogurt Chicken, 27
 Spicy Fried Fish, 28

VEGETARIAN DISHES, 29
 Spiced Rice, 29
 Carrots with Grated Coconut, 31
 Potatoes and Peas, 33

Pumpkin Curry, 34

DAL, 37
 Lentils with Garlic and Onion, 37
 Curried Chickpeas, 38

RAITA, 39
 Yogurt and Bananas, 39
 Yogurt with Cucumber and Mint, 41
 Yogurt with Cucumber and
  Tomato, 41

CHUTNEY, 42
 Fresh Coriander Chutney, 42
 Apple Chutney, 43

BREAD, 44
 Unleavened Whole Wheat Bread, 44
 Deep-Fried Whole Wheat Bread, 45

BEVERAGES, 46
 Spiced Tea, 46
 Salty Yogurt Drink, 47

THE CAREFUL COOK, 48

METRIC CONVERSION CHART, 49

INDEX, 49

Saffron

Indus River

Amritsar •

Corn

Himalayas

Delhi •

New Delhi •

Agra •

Millet

Lucknow •

Kanpur •

Lentils

Tea

Brahmaputra River

Ganges River

Pineapples

Sugar Cane

Ahmadabad •

Herring

Peanuts

Goats

Sheep

Vindhya Range

Grain

Mangoes

Calcutta •

Rice

Jute

Turmeric

Bombil (Bombay duck)

Bombay •

Cotton

Chilies

Godavari River

Bay of Bengal

Sardines

Hyderabad •

Krishna River

Tobacco

Prawns

Western Ghats

Pomfret

Eastern Ghats

Herring

Coconuts

Bangalore •

Arabian Sea

Bananas

Kaveri

Madras •

Oysters

River

Mackerel

Pepper

Cattle

Indian Ocean

Flag of India

INTRODUCTION

There are many countries in the world that include within their borders extreme contrasts in geography, climate, and population. Nowhere, however, do these contrasts seem so extreme as in India. Within the territory of this vast country are dense forests, arid deserts, fertile plains stretching for thousands of miles, humid tropical coasts fringed with tall coconut palms, and snow-covered peaks of some of the world's highest mountains. The weather during a typical Indian year includes scorching heat, with temperatures up to 120° F (49° C), and drenching monsoon rains that bring renewed life to the parched soil and make a large umbrella an essential part of everyone's daily wardrobe.

THE PEOPLE OF INDIA

The people of India, like the land they live in, are remarkably varied. Most Indians who live in the southern part of the country belong to a dark-skinned ethnic group. They are descendents of the earliest inhabitants of India, who created a rich civilization in the Indus River valley around 2500 B.C. The light-skinned people of northern India are descended from later invaders who pushed the original inhabitants south as they established their own powerful empires.

Modern Indians vary greatly not only in their ancestry but also in their styles of living. In both the north and south, many Indians make their homes in tiny rural villages centered around a single well and lighted only with kerosene lanterns. Others, however, live in cities like Bombay and Calcutta that are among the largest in the world, with some of the largest slums. Most Indians are farmers who raise crops for their own use, but some run large businesses, teach at universities, or work in a motion picture industry that produces hundreds of films each year.

A common language is often a unifying factor in a country with a large and diverse population, but in India, language tends to keep people apart rather than bringing them together. The 750 million inhabitants of India speak 14 major languages and more than 1,000 minor ones. Hindi is the official language of the country, but many Indians know it only as a second language, as English-speaking people might know Spanish or French. With their families and friends, they speak Bengali, Punjabi, Tamil, Telugu, or some other ancient tongue with its own tradition and literature.

Religion is another factor that separates Indians from each other and creates significant differences in their lives. India has two major religions, Hinduism and Islam, as well as several important smaller religious groups. About 83 percent of the Indian population are Hindus, people who honor the many gods and observe the complex laws of this ancient faith. Muslims, followers of the religion established by the prophet Muhammed, make up 11 percent of the population.

Both Hinduism and Islam are religions that involve a whole way of life. Rules governing diet, styles of dress, marriage and family life, and even occupations are part of the religious teachings accepted by devout Hindus and Muslims. Although some modern Indians no longer observe all the rules of their ancient faiths, many are still guided in their daily lives by the religious traditions of their ancestors.

THE VARIED TRADITIONS OF INDIAN FOOD

The food of India clearly—and deliciously—reflects the great variety of Indian life. In the different regions of this large country, what people eat depends on many different factors: the crops raised in the area, the ethnic and religious traditions of the inhabitants, the simplicity or sophistication of their life styles. All these variations have created a cuisine that is among the most fascinating and unique in the world.

The variations of geography and climate in India have an important influence on Indian foods. Northern India, with its wide plains and generally dry climate, produces large quantities of wheat. *Chapatis* and *puris*, breads made from wheat flour, are a staple of the diet in this region. The basic food of southern India is the rice that grows so well in the area's humid climate. Seafood, too, is typical of the south, with its miles of coastline, as well as tropical fruits like bananas and coconuts.

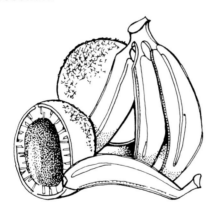

Other differences in eating habits are related to the different ethnic and religious traditions of India's people. Northern India has many Muslim inhabitants, whereas the people of the south are primarily Hindu. This difference in religious heritage affects the foods eaten in these areas. Muslims are forbidden by their religion to eat any pork or pork product, but they are allowed to have beef and other kinds of meat. Hindus never eat beef because the cow is considered a sacred animal in their faith. Many devout Hindus eat no meat at all; they are strict vegetarians, avoiding even seafood and eggs.

Fascinating variations in diet also stem from the historical backgrounds of northern and southern India. Over the long years of Indian history, the northern part of the country has been invaded many times by people from parts of central Asia. These invaders brought with them not only their Muslim faith but also a distinctive style of cooking. Today northern Indians still cook in this style, preparing many delicious dishes containing lamb, yogurt, and other ingredients commonly used in the Muslim countries of the Middle East.

Because invaders seldom made it as far as southern India, the people of the South preserved more of their early culture than their northern neighbors. The food of this region, with its emphasis on fresh-cooked vegetables and strong spices, represents classic Indian cooking at its finest.

Many spices are used in Indian cooking including:

1. green chili 2. garlic 3. whole cloves 4. coriander seed 5. cardamom pods 6. peppercorns (black) 7. fresh ginger 8. cumin seed 9. fenugreek seed 10. mustard seed 11. fresh coriander leaves 12. ground coriander 13. cayenne pepper 14. turmeric 15. ground cumin 16. ground cinnamon 17. stick cinnamon

SPICES: SWEET, HOT, SAVORY

Although there are many variations in the cooking of India, there are also some things that most Indian dishes have in common. One of the most important is the use of an exciting and unique assortment of spices. The spices of India have been famous for centuries. When Europeans first ventured into this part of the world, they came seeking the fabulous spices of the Indies: pepper, cinnamon, saffron, ginger, cloves. Today many of these spices and others equally exotic are used almost daily by every Indian household, no matter how poor.

Because spices are so important to Indian cooking, they are treated in a very special way. Most Indian cooks do not use already ground spices as cooks in western countries do. Instead the spices are bought whole from the spice market and ground by hand in small amounts for daily use.

Among people of western countries, Indian spices have the reputation of being hot, causing Indian food to burn the tongue and require large glasses of cold water to wash down.

Actually, most of the seasoning used in Indian cooking is not hot. Spices like cumin, coriander, and turmeric have a rich, mellow taste with only a mild bite to them.

What does give Indian food its heat are chilies, the same fiery red and green peppers that are used in Mexican cooking. Chilies are as popular in Indian kitchens as they are in Latin American ones. Most Indians enjoy the tangy taste that they give to any dish. If you don't share this fondness for hot food, you can cut down on the amount of chilies or leave them out altogether in preparing Indian dishes. This will not affect the wonderful flavor of the unique Indian spices.

A PASSAGE TO INDIA

Not many Westerners have an opportunity to travel in India and get a first-hand look at its rich and varied culture. Preparing and eating Indian foods, however, is one way to become acquainted with this fabulous country without ever leaving home. The recipes in this book will get you started on a voyage of discovery that you will never forget.

A stand in an Indian market displays a mouth-watering selection of fresh fruits and vegetables.

BEFORE YOU BEGIN

Cooking the Indian way requires some ingredients that are probably not on your kitchen shelf. Many of them can be found in large supermarkets in most parts of the United States. A few, however, are sold only in specialty shops that handle Indian or other kinds of ethnic foods. Let's take a look at the shopping list you will need for the recipes in this book.

SPECIAL INGREDIENTS

Pulses include peas, beans, and lentils, a very important category of food in India. Many Indian pulses are not available in the United States or western Europe, but the ones used in these recipes can be obtained at supermarkets or specialty stores. Dried brown *lentils* and *chickpeas* are sold at most large grocery stores. (Chickpeas are also known by their Spanish name, *garbanzo beans;* they can sometimes be found canned in the section of a supermarket specializing in Mexican food.)

Stores that carry Indian or Middle Eastern foods will have **split red lentils.** You may also find these mild-flavored lentils at a health-food store or cooperative grocery.

Spices and seasonings, as we have seen, make Indian cooking really special, so it is worthwhile to try and get the ones needed for the recipes you are preparing. The most common Indian spices—*cumin, coriander,* and *turmeric*—are available in large supermarkets already ground. Cumin and coriander seeds can often be found too, as well as **cardamom pods,** another whole spice used in Indian cooking. *Mustard seed* and *stick cinnamon* are usually on the supermarket spice shelf, and fresh *ginger* can be obtained in the produce department, along with the *garlic* that is as important in many Indian dishes as it is in Italian and French cooking.

Some Indian spices and seasonings may be difficult to find unless you go to an Indian grocery or a store that specializes in spices. Among these are *fenugreek* (seeds or powder) and *curry leaves.* The recipes in this book include only small amounts of these special ingredients, and they can be omitted without changing the basic taste of the dishes.

Fresh coriander is a green herb that is used to add flavor and color to many Indian dishes. Under the name *cilantro,* it is also popular in Mexican cooking. Some large supermarkets now carry fresh coriander in their produce departments, right next to the parsley. Mexican and Oriental grocery stores also sell the herb. Try to get fresh coriander if you can. Parsley can be substituted in some dishes, but the taste will be quite different.

Chilies are what make Indian food hot, and you will want to try at least one dish that includes these spicy relatives of the familiar green or bell pepper. There are several forms of chilies used in this book. The most common is the fresh *green chili,* a slim, bright-green pepper that can often be obtained in the produce department of a large supermarket. Green chilies can also be found canned in the Mexican food section of many groceries.

Another form of chili that you will need is *cayenne pepper,* which is not pepper at all but dried red chilies that have been ground to make a fine powder. (Black pepper comes from an entirely different plant.)

Rice, one of India's most important foods, is often cultivated by hand.

Coconut, sweet, white, and fragrant, is an important ingredient in many dishes from southern India. The kitchen equipment of a southern Indian cook often includes a special utensil used to scrape the delicious coconut meat from the inside of the hard shell. Since coconuts are not readily available in North America, the recipes in this book use prepared coconut products. Unsweetened *flaked coconut* can usually be obtained in a cooperative grocery or a health-food store. The flaked coconut carried in most supermarkets is flavored with sugar, but it can be used if the unsweetened variety is not available. You may have to get canned *coconut milk* at a store that specializes in Indian or Oriental food. If it isn't available, coconut milk can be made from flaked coconut. (Directions on page 35.)

COOKING UTENSILS

colander— A bowl-shaped dish with holes used for washing or draining food

electric grinder— A small electric appliance used for grinding hard, dry foods such as spices, coffee beans, and grains

sieve—A bowl-shaped utensil made of wire mesh used to wash or drain small, fine foods such as loose tea or rice

skewer—A thin metal or wood rod used to hold small pieces of food for broiling or grilling

slotted spoon—A spoon with small openings in the bowl used to pick solid food out of a liquid

spatula—A flat, thin utensil, usually metal, used to lift, toss, turn, or scoop food

wok—A steel, aluminum, or cast iron pot with a rounded bottom and sloping sides used for deep-frying, stir-frying, and steaming

COOKING TERMS

beat—To stir rapidly in a circular motion

boil—To heat a liquid until bubbles form and rise rapidly to the surface

fillet—A boneless piece of fish or meat

garnish—To decorate with small pieces of food

knead—To work dough by pressing it with the palms, pushing it outward, and then pressing it over on itself

paste—A soft, creamy mixture of ground foods

roast—To cook in an open pan in an oven so heat penetrates the food from all sides

rub—To mix solid fat into flour until it has a coarse, mealy texture

simmer—To cook over low heat in a liquid kept just below the boiling point

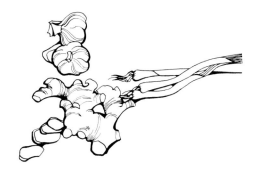

Before you start cooking, carefully read through the recipe you want to try from beginning to end. Now you are ready to shop for ingredients and to organize the cookware you will need. Once you have assembled everything, you can begin to cook. Before you start, it is also very important to read *The Careful Cook* on page 48.

PREPARING INDIAN FOODS

Most of the cooking methods used in India are well known to western cooks, but some of the methods of preparing the ingredients for the dishes may be unfamiliar. This is particularly true of the way that Indians treat spices.

PREPARING SPICES One thing that you will discover when you try some of the recipes in this book is that they call for whole spices like cumin seed or cardamom pods to be heated or cooked in hot oil before being added to the other ingredients. Indians believe that such cooking brings out a different flavor than when ground spices or whole uncooked spices are used.

When dishes call for ground spices, Indian cooks always grind them fresh rather than using pre-ground ones. In preparing these recipes, you can use already ground spices from the supermarket, but you should at least try grinding whole spices to experience the marvelous flavor they give to Indian dishes.

The easiest method of grinding whole spices is to use a small electric grinder of the kind used to grind coffee beans or nuts. (An electric blender can also be used, although the mixture will not be as fine.) You should start with about the same amount of whole spice as the amount of ground spice called for in the recipe. For example, if the recipe calls for ½ teaspoon of ground cumin, put ½ teaspoon of cumin seed in your grinder. Grind for about 30 seconds or until the mixture is as fine as ground cinnamon.

Indian cooks often combine their fresh-ground spices into special blends called *garam masalas.* These spice mixtures are usually added to dishes near the end of the cooking or used as a garnish. Each cook has his or her own recipe for *garam masala,* but most contain some combination of cumin, cardamom, cinnamon, and cloves. On page 24, you will find a recipe for one of these savory spice mixtures.

INDIAN MEALS

Considering the great variety of Indian food and styles of eating, it is not surprising that there is no one pattern for daily meals in India. What people eat at different times of day depends on where they live, on the religious laws they observe, on whether they are poor or rich. In general, however, most Indians have one main meal a day, usually between 12 and 2 P.M., and several smaller meals. Breakfast may consist of lentils and bread or yogurt, always accompanied by tea. Afternoon tea is a custom in many parts of India, and most Indians also enjoy snacking on salty, highly seasoned treats sold by street vendors. The day ends with a light evening meal of several simple dishes—for example, rice and lentils—usually eaten after 8 P.M.

For most Indians, the big meal of the day consists of small portions of many dishes instead of one main dish. This is particularly true for vegetarians, who eat only vegetables fixed in various delicious ways, usually accompanied by rice. Non-vegetarians may have one meat dish (if they can afford it), along with vegetables, lentils, a salad like *raita,* and bread or rice. Desserts are not usually included in daily meals, but on special occasions, Indians enjoy eating candylike sweets made from milk.

According to Indian custom, the main recipes in this book are divided into vegetarian and non-vegetarian categories. You will also find recipes for accompanying dishes like chutneys, breads, *raitas*, and pulses (lentils and peas) that could be eaten with both kinds of meals. For your first taste of Indian food, you might choose just one dish, for example, spicy fried fish, and serve it with a vegetable and a green salad. If you would like to try a simple vegetarian meal, pumpkin curry over plain rice, curried chickpeas, and cucumber-mint *raita* would make a good combination. For a meat meal, start out with *samosas* and coriander chutney, then serve your guests yogurt chicken, carrots with coconut, banana *raita*, and *puris*.

If you would like to eat your Indian meal in the Indian style, have your guests sit on the floor and give each person a tray with small dishes containing individual portions of the various foods. Indians usually don't use forks and spoons; they eat with their fingers, using pieces of bread to scoop up food with sauces or mixing them with rice. It takes practice to eat neatly with your fingers, but Indians say that food tastes much better this way. If you would like to give it a try, be sure to have wet cloths or fingerbowls handy.

AN INDIAN MENU

Below is a list of Indian foods from which typical daily menus can be made. The Hindi names of the dishes are also given, along with a guide on how to pronounce them. All of the recipes for these foods are included in the book.

ENGLISH	HINDI	PRONUNCIATION GUIDE
Spices	*Masala*	muh-SAH-lah
Mixed Spices	Garam Masala	GAR-um muh-SAH-lah
Meat and Fish Dishes	*Amish Bhojan*	ah-MISH BO-jun
Deep-Fried Stuffed Savory Pastries	Samosas	sah-MO-sahz
Spiced Ground Meat	Kheema	KEE-muh
Ground Lamb Kebabs	Kabab Masala	kuh-BAHB muh-SAH-lah
Yogurt Chicken	Murg Dahi	MURG DAH-hee
Spicy Fried Fish	Muchli Masala	MUCH-lee muh-SAH-lah
Vegetarian Dishes	*Niramish Bhojan*	NEER-ah-mish BO-jun
Spiced Rice	Pulao	puh-LAO
Carrots with Grated Coconut	Gajar Nariyal	GUH-juhr NUHR-ee-yuhl
Potatoes and Peas	Aloo Mattar	AH-loo MUH-tahr
Pumpkin "Curry"	Sambar	SAHM-bar
Pulses	*Dal*	dahl
Lentils with Garlic and Onion	Masoor Dal	muh-SOOR dahl
Curried Chickpeas	Channa Dal	CHUHN-uh dahl

ENGLISH	HINDI	PRONUNCIATION GUIDE
	Raita	RI-tah
Yogurt and Bananas	Kela ka Raita	KEE-lah kah RI-tah
Yogurt with Cucumber and Mint	Kheera ka Raita	KEER-ah kah RI-tah
Yogurt with Cucumber and Tomato	Kheera-Tamatar Raita	KEER-ah tuh-MAH-tuhr RI-tah
Chutney	*Chatni*	CHUT-nee
Fresh Coriander Chutney	Dhanya Chatni	DAH-nee-yah CHUT-nee
Apple Chutney	Sheb ke Chatni	SHEB kee CHUT-nee
Bread	*Roti*	ROE-tee
Unleavened Whole Wheat Bread	Chapatis	chuh-PAH-tees
Deep-Fried Whole Wheat Bread	Puris	POO-rees
Beverages	*Pinay ke Liye*	PIH-nay kay LEE-ay
Spiced Tea	Masala Chai	muh-SAH-lah CHI
Salty Yogurt Drink	Lassi	LUH-see

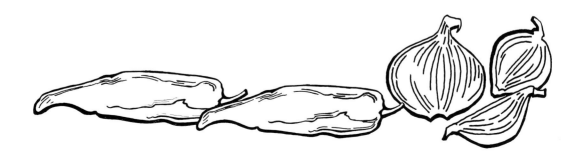

In simple kitchens such as this, Indian cooks prepare a great variety of appetizing dishes.

MEAT AND FISH DISHES

Deep-Fried Stuffed Savory Pastries/ Samosas

Samosas are a favorite snack food in India. These little pastries are perfect for eating with your fingers and make a good appetizer to start an Indian meal. Samosas can be stuffed with many kinds of meat or vegetable fillings. Kheema (page 23) makes a spicy meat filling. For vegetarian samosas, fill the pastries with potatoes and peas (page 33). Coriander chutney (page 42) is a good dipping sauce for any kind of samosa.

Dough:

½ **cup all-purpose flour**
½ **cup whole-wheat flour**
¼ **teaspoon salt**
1 **tablespoon butter or margarine**

up to ¼ cup water
about 1 cup vegetable oil (for frying)
about 2 cups filling

1. Put flour and salt in a mixing bowl. Cut butter into small pieces and add to flour. Rub butter into flour with your fingertips until mixture looks like large bread crumbs. Mix in enough water, a little at a time, to form a firm dough.
2. Knead dough in bowl for about 2 or 3 minutes or until smooth. Cover bowl and refrigerate while making filling.
3. Remove dough from refrigerator and place on a floured surface. Knead dough for about 5 minutes.
4. Divide dough into pieces about the size of walnuts, and roll each piece into a smooth ball with your hands.
5. On a floured surface, roll balls into thin rounds with a rolling pin. Cut each round in half.
6. Put about 1 tablespoon filling onto a piece of dough. Fold dough over filling to form a triangle. Seal edges of dough with your fingers and then with the tines of a fork. Continue making *samosas.*

7. In a medium saucepan with deep sides or a wok, heat oil over medium-high heat. (Oil should be deep enough to cover *samosas* while cooking.) Carefully place one *samosa* in oil. If *samosa* fries to a golden brown in about 3 minutes, the oil is at the right temperature. If it takes longer than this, increase temperature of oil. When oil is at the right temperature, continue frying *samosas,* a few at a time, for 3 minutes each. Remove *samosas* with a slotted spoon and drain on paper towels. Eat hot or at room temperature.

Makes 10 to 15 samosas

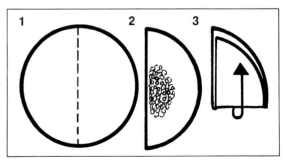

1. Roll dough into circle and cut in half. 2. Place filling on dough. 3. Fold dough over filling to form triangle, then seal.

A mixture of whole and ground spices combine to make *kheema* both sweet and savory.

Spiced Ground Meat/ Kheema

Kheema *is a very popular dish all over northern India. In the cities, it is sold at stands in the streets and often eaten as a quick snack or lunch. In its basic ingredients,* kheema *is similar to the hamburger casseroles often served in Western homes, but the Indian spices give it a wonderfully special flavor.*

1 **pound ground lamb or beef**
1 **tablespoon** *garam masala* **(see page 24) or 1 teaspoon each pepper, ground clove, and ground cumin**
½ **teaspoon salt**
3 **tablespoons vegetable oil**
½ **medium onion, thinly sliced**
3 **cloves garlic, chopped**
1 **tablespoon chopped fresh ginger**
3 **cardamom pods**
1 **stick cinnamon**
2 **medium potatoes, peeled and chopped**
1 **cup water**
1 **green chili, chopped**
2 **medium tomatoes, chopped**
1 **10-ounce package frozen peas, thawed or 1 17-ounce can green peas, drained**
fresh coriander for garnish

1. In a bowl, mix together meat, *garam masala,* and salt.
2. Heat oil in a large skillet over medium-high heat. Add onion, garlic, ginger, cardamom, and cinnamon and fry about 5 minutes or until onions turn brown. Add meat mixture and stir until meat is completely brown.
3. Add potatoes and water, lower heat, and simmer about 20 minutes or until potatoes are tender and liquid has cooked off.
4. Add chili, tomatoes, and peas and stir to combine. Cook for about 5 minutes to heat through.
5. Remove skillet from heat. Remove cardamom and cinnamon from skillet. Garnish *kheema* with coriander leaves and serve steaming hot.

Serves 6 to 8

Garam Masala

3 sticks cinnamon
½ cup cardamom pods
¼ cup whole cloves
¼ cup cumin seeds
2 tablespoons coriander seeds
¼ cup black peppercorns
1 tablespoon ground ginger

1. Preheat oven to 200°. Place all ingredients except ginger in a 9- by 13-inch baking pan. Put pan on bottom oven rack and roast for 30 minutes. Stir spices several times so they roast evenly.

2. Remove pan from oven and let stand for 5 minutes or until spices are cool enough to handle.

3. Use your fingers to break open cardamom pods. Remove seeds and discard pods.

4. With a rolling pin, crush the cinnamon sticks between two towels or in a plastic bag.

5. Combine all spices except ginger in a bowl and mix well.

6. Grind the spice mixture, a little at a time, in an electric grinder or blender. (If you use an electric blender, your *garam masala* will be fairly coarse.)

7. Add ground ginger to the spice mixture and mix well.

8. Put *garam masala* in a jar with a tight-fitting lid and store at room temperature. (*Garam masala* will stay fresh for up to 6 months if kept in an airtight container.)

Makes 1 cup

Ground Lamb Kebabs/ Kabab Masala

Kebabs, meats cooked on skewers, are eaten throughout northern India, as they are in the Muslim countries of the Middle East. This recipe uses ground lamb or beef that is molded around the skewers and broiled. Kebabs are also delicious when cooked over a charcoal grill.

1½ **pounds ground lamb or beef**
3 **cloves garlic, chopped**
1 **teaspoon grated fresh ginger**
1 **green chili, finely chopped**
1 **medium onion, finely chopped**
3 **tablespoons chopped fresh coriander leaves**
1 **tablespoon plain yogurt (optional)**
½ **teaspoon ground turmeric**
½ **teaspoon ground cumin**
1 **tablespoon lemon juice**
1 **teaspoon salt**
1 **tablespoon butter or margarine, melted**

1. In a large bowl, combine all ingredients except melted butter. With your hands, mix ingredients well until mixture is fairly stiff. Cover bowl and let stand at room temperature for 30 minutes.
2. Preheat broiler. Lightly grease 12 skewers with the melted butter. Wet hands slightly and shape small pieces of meat mixture into oblong shapes around skewers, making two kebabs on each skewer.
3. Line the bottom of a broiler pan with aluminum foil. Place skewers across broiler pan.
4. Place broiler pan in oven about 6 inches from heat. Broil kebabs for about 5 minutes or until well browned. Turn skewers and broil kebabs for an additional 4 minutes.
5. Place skewers on a platter and serve.

Serves 4 to 6

For a typical northern Indian meal, serve your guests flavorful yogurt chicken *(left)* **and** *pulao,* **rice studded with raisins, nuts, and whole spices** *(right).*

Yogurt Chicken/ Murg Dahi

Yogurt gives this dish from northern India a wonderful flavor and also makes the meat very tender. The yogurt and spice flavors will penetrate the chicken if you skin it as Indian cooks always do. Just hold a chicken piece in one hand and pull hard on the loose skin with the other hand. A paper towel will help you to get a good grip.

3½ to 4 pounds chicken pieces, skinned
  1 teaspoon salt
  1 green chili, finely chopped
  1 cup (8 ounces) plain yogurt
  ¼ cup chopped fresh coriander leaves
  1 tablespoon chopped fresh ginger
  3 or 4 cloves garlic, chopped
  ¼ cup (½ stick) butter or margarine, melted

1. Prick chicken pieces all over with a fork and place in a large bowl. In a small bowl, combine salt, chili, yogurt, coriander leaves, ginger, and garlic, and mix well. Pour over chicken, cover bowl, and refrigerate for 6 hours or overnight.

2. To cook chicken, preheat oven to 400°. Pour half the melted butter into a roasting pan. Put chicken into pan and pour yogurt mixture on top. Place pan in middle of oven and roast for about 20 minutes. Reduce heat to 350° and continue roasting, basting frequently with remaining butter and pan juices, for about 30 minutes or until chicken is done.

3. Remove chicken and place on a serving platter. Pour sauce over chicken and serve immediately.

Serves 4 to 6

Spicy Fried Fish/
Muchli Masala

India's coastal waters produce many fish like pomfret that are not found in other parts of the world. For this tasty fish recipe, you can use sole, haddock, or other common kinds of white fish. Spicy fried fish is a dish from southern India, and it uses what is called a "wet" masala, spices mixed with water or other liquids to form a paste. South Indian cooks often prepare their spices in this way instead of using a mixture of dry spices.

2 pounds white-fish fillets, fresh or frozen
2 cloves garlic, chopped
1 teaspoon salt
1 teaspoon grated fresh ginger
½ teaspoon ground turmeric
½ teaspoon black pepper
¼ teaspoon cayenne pepper
2 teaspoons lemon juice
¼ cup vegetable oil (for frying)

1. Rinse fish under cool running water and pat dry with paper towels.
2. In a small bowl, combine garlic, salt, ginger, turmeric, and peppers with lemon juice. Stir to form a paste.
3. Rub paste on both sides of fish fillets and let stand uncovered at room temperature for 20 minutes.
4. In a heavy skillet, heat oil over medium-high heat. Carefully add fish to skillet. Fry fish about 5 minutes or until bottom side is golden. With a spatula, turn fish and fry other side about 5 minutes or until golden.
5. Place fish on platter and garnish with fresh coriander or parsley and lemon wedges.

Serves 4

VEGETARIAN DISHES

Spiced Rice/Pulao

This rice dish from northern India is similiar to the pilafs popular in Middle Eastern countries. It is a tasty combination of rice with spices, raisins, and nuts. The best kind of Indian rice is basmati, *a long-grained rice with a delicate, nutty flavor. If you can use* basmati *in your* pulao, *it will be really special.*

⅓ **cup vegetable or peanut oil**
½ **medium onion, thinly sliced**
5 **whole cloves**
½ **stick cinnamon**
5 **cardamom pods**
½ **teaspoon ground coriander**
1 **cup *basmati* or other long-grain rice, rinsed and well-drained**
½ **teaspoon salt**
2 **cups boiling water**
1 **tablespoon butter or margarine**
¼ **cup raisins**
2 **tablespoons blanched slivered almonds or cashews**

1. In a heavy saucepan, heat oil over medium-high heat. Add onion and cook about 5 minutes or until soft.
2. Add cloves, cinnamon, cardamom, and coriander. Reduce heat to medium-low and cook for 1 minute. Stir in rice and fry until rice has been well coated with oil.
3. Add salt and boiling water and bring mixture to a boil over medium heat.
4. When rice begins to boil, cover pan, reduce heat to very low, and cook rice for about 15 minutes or until all water is absorbed and rice is tender.
5. When rice is cooked, heat butter in a small skillet over medium-high heat. Add raisins and nuts and fry for 1 or 2 minutes or until raisins are plump and nuts are golden brown.
6. Stir raisin-nut mixture into rice and serve immediately. (Don't forget that there are whole spices in this that you will want to remove before eating.)

Serves 6 to 8

Carrots take on a new appeal when they are combined with sweet grated coconut and tangy mustard seeds.

Carrots with Grated Coconut/
Gajar Nariyal

This simple vegetable dish uses black mustard seeds, which have a more delicate flavor than the ordinary yellow seeds. Yellow mustard seeds can be used if you can't get black ones, but you might want to use only ½ teaspoon instead.

6 carrots, peeled and cut into thin round slices
½ cup grated coconut
1 teaspoon ground cumin
2 teaspoons ground coriander
2 teaspoons ground turmeric
5 tablespoons vegetable oil
1 teaspoon black mustard seed
¾ cup water
¼ cup ground peanuts (optional)

1. In a bowl, combine carrots, coconut, cumin, coriander, and turmeric and mix well.

2. In a skillet, heat oil over medium-high heat. Add mustard seed and fry for about 3 minutes or until seeds pop. (Keep lid near skillet so seeds don't pop out.)
3. Add carrot-coconut mixture and fry for 10 minutes. Add water, lower heat, and simmer for about 10 minutes or until carrots are tender.
4. Mix ground peanuts into carrots and serve steaming hot.

Serves 4 to 6

Potatoes and peas are commonly eaten in northern India, where the cool climate is suitable for growing these vegetables.

Potatoes and Peas/
Aloo Mattar

This savory mixture of potatoes and peas can be eaten as part of a vegetarian meal or served with chapatis *as a lunch or snack. It also makes an excellent filling for* samosas.

2 tablespoons vegetable or peanut oil
1 green chili, chopped
1 teaspoon chopped fresh ginger
1 clove garlic, chopped
1 small onion, chopped
½ teaspoon salt
3 large potatoes, peeled and chopped
2 cups water
1 10-ounce package frozen peas,
   thawed or 1 17-ounce can green
   peas, drained
¼ cup cashews for garnish

1. In a large skillet, heat oil over medium-high heat. Add chili, ginger, garlic, onion, and salt and fry about 3 minutes, stirring frequently, or until mixture is brown and fragrant.

2. Add potatoes and water and stir to combine. Cover skillet, lower heat, and simmer about 20 minutes or until potatoes are tender.

3. When potatoes are cooked, add peas and simmer 2 or 3 minutes or until peas are heated through.

4. Serve potatoes and peas hot or at room temperature with cashews sprinkled on top.

Serves 4 to 6

Savory pumpkin curry is typical of the highly spiced dishes popular in southern India.

Pumpkin Curry/
Sambar

The Indian "curry" served in most western countries is usually a rice dish covered with a thick, yellow sauce containing commercial curry powder. In authentic Indian cooking, there is no specific dish called curry, but there are many dishes with sauces, each made with its own special spices and ingredients. The delicious sauce of pumpkin curry is made with coconut milk and lentils.

If you can't get fresh pumpkin, try making this southern Indian specialty with a winter squash like acorn or hubbard.

½ **cup coconut milk**
1 **small pumpkin or winter squash
    (about 3 cups chopped)**
1 **cup lentils, brown or split red**
1 **teaspoon cayenne pepper**
½ **teaspoon ground cumin**
¼ **teaspoon ground turmeric**
½ **teaspoon salt**
½ **cup water**

1 tablespoon vegetable oil
¼ teaspoon ground fenugreek seed
¼ teaspoon black mustard seed
1 large onion, thinly sliced
1 curry leaf (optional)

1. If you can't get canned coconut milk, put ½ cup flaked coconut in an electric blender. Add ½ cup boiling water and blend for 1 minute. Place mixture in a sieve over a bowl and press on coconut with the back of a spoon to get all the liquid out. Set coconut milk aside and discard grated coconut. (If you do not have an electric blender, soak coconut in hot water for 5 minutes before straining.)
2. **For pumpkin**, cut into quarters, scrape out seeds, cut off peel, and chop into 1-inch squares. **For squash**, first bake whole for 20 minutes on the middle rack of a 400° oven. Cool, then quarter, scrape out seeds, cut off peel, and chop.
3. Place lentils in a colander and rinse thoroughly with cold water. Remove any inedible objects from lentils while washing.
4. Put 4 cups of water in a large saucepan.

Add cayenne pepper, cumin, turmeric, and salt and bring to a boil. Add lentils, cover, and lower heat. Simmer for about 30 minutes or until lentils are tender. (If you are using split red lentils, they will cook in about 15 to 20 minutes.)
5. Add pumpkin squares to lentils. Cover and simmer 15 to 20 minutes or until pumpkin is tender.
6. Add coconut milk to kettle and stir. As soon as mixture begins to boil, remove from heat and set aside.
7. In a skillet, heat oil over medium-high heat. Add fenugreek, mustard seed, onion slices, and curry leaf and fry for 4 or 5 minutes or until mixture is brown.
8. Add onion-and-spice mixture to kettle. Cover kettle and let stand 5 minutes.
9. Stir pumpkin curry before serving over rice.

Serves 6 to 8

Channna dal (left) or *masoor dal (right)* can be teamed with yogurt and *chapatis* to make a simple but nourishing meal.

DAL

Dal *is the Hindi word for pulses, those versatile beans, lentils, and peas that are such an important part of the Indian diet. Most Indians have some kind of* dal *at almost every meal. Eaten with a starchy food like bread or rice and a milk product like yogurt, they form the basis of a well-balanced diet. The simple* dal *recipe on this page uses brown lentils or split red lentils, known in Hindi as* masoor dal. *On the following page is a recipe for a hearty dish of chickpeas, or* channa dal. *In preparing any* dal, *be sure to examine the pulses for small stones, twigs, and other inedible objects before cooking them.*

Lentils with Garlic and Onion/
Masoor Dal

3 cups water
1 cup split red or brown lentils, washed and drained

½ teaspoon ground turmeric
⅛ teaspoon cayenne pepper (optional)
3 tablespoons vegetable or peanut oil
½ teaspoon whole cumin seed
3 cloves garlic, finely chopped
1 medium onion, chopped
1 teaspoon salt

1. Combine water, lentils, turmeric, and cayenne in a medium saucepan and bring to a boil over medium-high heat. Cover pan, turn heat to low, and simmer for about 30 minutes or until lentils are tender. (If you are using split red lentils, they will cook in about 15 to 20 minutes.)
2. Meanwhile, in another saucepan, heat vegetable oil over medium heat. Add cumin seed and stir. Add garlic, onion, and salt and continue stirring for about 5 minutes or until onion begins to brown.
3. When lentils are cooked, add onion mixture to them. Mix well and simmer for 5 additional minutes before serving.

Serves 6 to 8

Curried Chickpeas/
Channa Dal

**1½ cups (12 ounces) chickpeas,
　　washed and drained
5 cups water
1 teaspoon ground turmeric
½ teaspoon ground cumin
1 teaspoon ground coriander
½ teaspoon cayenne pepper (optional)
3 tablespoons butter or margarine
1 teaspoon cumin seed
1 medium onion, chopped
1 clove garlic, chopped
1 tablespoon grated fresh ginger
1 teaspoon *garam masala* (optional)
2 tablespoons chopped fresh
　　coriander leaves**

1. Put chickpeas in a bowl. Add enough cold water to cover and soak overnight.
2. To cook, drain chickpeas. Place chickpeas, water, turmeric, cumin, coriander, and cayenne in a heavy saucepan and bring to a boil over medium-high heat. Reduce heat to low, cover pan, and simmer for about 1 hour.
3. In a large saucepan, melt butter over medium heat. Add cumin seed and cook for 1 minute. Add the onion, garlic, and ginger and cook for about 5 minutes, stirring frequently, or until onion turns golden brown.
4. Add chickpeas and cooking liquid to onion mixture. Turn heat to high and bring to a boil, stirring constantly. Cover pan, reduce heat to low, and simmer 30 minutes or until chickpeas are tender but not mushy.
5. Add *garam masala* and mix well.
6. Place chickpeas in a serving dish and sprinkle with chopped coriander leaves.

Serves 6 to 8

RAITA

As an accompaniment to the spicy flavor of an Indian meal, nothing could be better than a raita, a cool and crunchy combination of yogurt with vegetables, fruits, and various seasonings. Indian cooks usually make their own yogurt out of water-buffalo milk. You can try making yogurt out of cow's milk (it's not that difficult), or simply use unflavored yogurt from the supermarket.

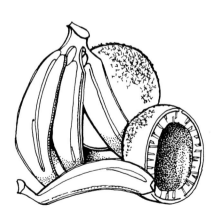

Yogurt and Bananas/ Kela ka Raita

1½ **cups (12 ounces) plain yogurt**
  2 **large bananas, peeled and sliced**
  ¼ **cup flaked coconut**
  1 **green chili, finely chopped**
  1 **teaspoon lemon juice**
  ½ **teaspoon *garam masala* or**
    ¼ **teaspoon each ground coriander and cinnamon**
  ¼ **teaspoon salt**
  1 **teaspoon finely chopped fresh coriander leaves**

1. In a medium mixing bowl, beat yogurt until smooth. Stir in bananas, coconut, chili, lemon juice, *garam masala*, and salt. Cover bowl and chill at least 1 hour.
2. Just before serving, sprinkle coriander leaves over raita.

Serves 4

Kheera-tamatar raita (left), kheera ka raita (center), and *kela ka raita (right)* are cool dishes ideal to serve on hot summer days or as an accompaniment to spicy food.

Yogurt with Cucumber and Mint/
Kheera ka Raita

3 cups (24 ounces) plain yogurt
1 medium cucumber, peeled and
   chopped
3 tablespoons finely chopped fresh
   mint leaves or 1 tablespoon dried
   mint
½ teaspoon ground cumin
1 teaspoon salt
¼ teaspoon black pepper
⅛ teaspoon cayenne pepper (optional)

1. In a medium mixing bowl, beat yogurt until smooth. Stir in remaining ingredients.
2. Cover bowl and chill at least 1 hour before serving.

Serves 6

Yogurt with Cucumber and Tomato/
Kheera-Tamatar Raita

1 medium tomato
1 medium cucumber, peeled
2 cups (16 ounces) plain yogurt
1 small onion, chopped
3 tablespoons chopped fresh
   coriander or parsley
½ teaspoon salt
½ teaspoon black pepper
   dash of cayenne pepper (optional)

1. Cut tomato in half and remove seeds. Chop tomato into small pieces.
2. Chop cucumber into small pieces.
3. In a bowl, beat yogurt until smooth. Combine yogurt with remaining ingredients and mix well.
4. Cover bowl and chill at least 1 hour before serving.

Serves 4

CHUTNEY/
Chatni

No Indian meal would be complete without a small serving of chutney, a spicy mixture of fresh or cooked vegetables or fruits designed to provide an accent to the main dishes. Chutneys are made out of many kinds of ingredients, and they have many different flavors—sweet, sour, mild, fiery. Fresh coriander chutney has the tangy, slighty sour taste of the green coriander leaves. This popular chutney is made fresh daily in many Indian households. Apple chutney is a sweet, cooked chutney that will keep for several weeks in the refrigerator.

Fresh Coriander Chutney/
Dhanya Chatni

3 cups fresh coriander leaves, coarsely chopped
½ green chili, chopped
2 tablespoons lemon juice
¼ teaspoon salt
½ teaspoon ground cumin
¼ teaspoon black pepper

1. Combine all ingredients in a blender and blend until smooth.
2. Put chutney in a small glass or non-metallic bowl to serve.

Makes ½ cup

Apple Chutney/
Sheb ki Chatni

3 tart cooking apples, peeled, cored,
      and coarsely chopped
1 cup chopped dried fruit such as
      peaches, apricots, and pears
½ cup golden raisins
3 cloves garlic, chopped
2 teaspoons finely chopped fresh
      ginger
1 teaspoon salt
¼ teaspoon cayenne pepper
1 cup white-wine vinegar
1½ cups sugar

1. In a heavy saucepan, combine all ingredients and mix well. Bring to a boil over medium-high heat.

2. Reduce heat and simmer for about 45 minutes, stirring occasionally, or until mixture is thick.

3. Remove saucepan from heat and cool chutney to room temperature.

4. Pour chutney into a non-metallic, covered container and refrigerate until ready to use.

Makes 3 cups

Sweet, pungent apple chutney is a combination of wonderful flavors and jewel-like colors.

BREAD/
Roti

The breads that Indians eat are very different from the plump, crusty loaves that are familiar to Westerners. Most Indian bread has no leavening agent like yeast, so it does not rise when it is cooked. Chapatis, *the most popular kind of Indian bread, are flat pancakes that look something like Mexican tortillas. Like tortillas, they are cooked on a very hot, ungreased griddle.* Puris *are made from the same whole wheat dough as* chapatis, *but they are deep-fried in oil so that they puff up. Both kinds of breads are best when eaten right after they are made.*

Unleavened Whole Wheat Bread/
Chapatis

2½ cups whole wheat flour
2 tablespoons butter or margarine
1 teaspoon salt
1 cup lukewarm water

1. Put 2 cups flour into a large mixing bowl.
2. Cut butter into small pieces. Make a hollow in the center of the flour and add butter. Rub butter into flour with your fingertips until mixture looks like large bread crumbs.
3. Mix salt into water. Add enough water, a little at a time, to flour mixture to make a firm (but not stiff) dough.
4. Knead dough in bowl for about 5 or 10 minutes. Cover bowl with a damp cloth and let stand at room temperature for at least 1 hour.
5. Divide dough into pieces about the size of walnuts, and roll each piece into a smooth ball with your hands.

6. Sprinkle remaining ½ cup flour onto a flat surface. With a rolling pin, roll out each ball until it resembles a thin pancake, about ⅛-inch thick.

7. Heat a heavy skillet or griddle over medium-high heat. When the skillet is hot, place one *chapati* in the center. When small brown spots appear on the bottom and the edges begin to curl up (in about 1 minute), turn the *chapati* over with a spatula. Cook *chapati* for about 2 minutes or until small brown spots appear on bottom.

8. Continue cooking *chapatis*, one at a time. Wrap the cooked ones in a towel to keep them warm.

9. Brush cooked *chapatis* with butter and serve warm.

Makes 12 to 15 chapatis

Deep-Fried Whole Wheat Bread/
Puris

whole wheat dough (recipe on p. 44)

1. Divide dough into pieces about the size of walnuts, and roll each piece into a smooth ball with your hands.

2. Sprinkle ½ cup flour on a flat surface. With a rolling pin, roll balls into thin rounds.

3. In a large skillet, heat oil over medium-high heat. Carefully place each *puri* in oil, one at a time. Using a spatula, carefully splash oil onto *puris* while frying. This will make *puris* puff up and will cook the top side of each one. Fry *puris* about 2 minutes or until golden brown on both sides.

4. Remove *puris* from skillet, drain on paper towels, and serve immediately.

Makes 15 to 20 puris

BEVERAGES/
Pinay ke Liye

Indians drink many kinds of beverages, some familiar and others that might seem exotic to Westerners. In large Indian cities, street vendors sell glasses of brightly colored sharbats, *sweet drinks made with sugar and various flavorings like mint and sandalwood. In southern India, coffee is the preferred beverage, and many households grind coffee beans fresh every day. Tea is grown in northern India, where it is often served spiced with cinnamon and cloves. Indian spiced tea makes a delicious hot drink on a cold winter day.*

Spiced Tea/
Masala Chai

3 cups water
2 sticks cinnamon
15 cardamom pods
15 whole cloves
1 tablespoon chopped fresh ginger
3 tablespoons black tea leaves
1 cup milk
3 tablespoons sugar

1. In a medium saucepan, bring water, cinnamon, cardamom, cloves, and ginger to a boil over medium-high heat. Turn off heat, add tea, and cover pan. Let stand for 3 minutes.
2. Strain tea-and-spice mixture into another saucepan. Add milk and sugar and bring to a boil over medium-high heat.
3. As soon as tea begins to boil, remove from heat and pour into cups. Serve immediately.

Serves 4 to 6

Salty Yogurt Drink/ Lassi

Lassi *is a uniquely Indian drink made with yogurt. Many Indians believe that a glass of creamy, salt-flavored* lassi *is the perfect beverage to drink with spicy foods.*

1 cup plain yogurt
2½ cups ice-cold water
1 teaspoon salt
1 teaspoon ground cumin
1 green chili, finely chopped (optional)

1. Combine all ingredients in blender and blend about 15 seconds or until frothy. (If you don't have a blender, place all ingredients in a tightly covered jar and shake to mix.)
2. Pour into glasses and serve immediately.
Serves 4 to 6

Two unusual Indian beverages: *Masala chai*, tea prepared with milk and spices *(bottom)*, and *lassi*, a yogurt drink with the tang of salt *(top)*

THE CAREFUL COOK

Whenever you cook, there are certain safety rules you must always keep in mind.

1. Always wash your hands before handling food.
2. Thoroughly wash all raw vegetables and fruits to remove dirt and chemicals.
3. Use a cutting board when cutting up vegetables and fruits. Don't cut them up in your hand! And be sure to cut in a direction *away* from you and your fingers.
4. Long hair or loose clothing can catch fire if brought near the burners of a stove. If you have long hair, tie it back before cooking.
5. Turn all pot handles toward the back of the stove so that you will not catch your sleeves or jewelry on them. This is especially important when younger brothers and sisters are around. They could easily knock off a pot and get burned.
6. Always use a pot holder to steady hot pots or to take pans out of the oven. Don't use a wet cloth on a hot pan because the steam it produces could burn you.

7. Lift the lid of a steaming pot with the opening away from you so that you will not get burned.
8. If you get burned, hold the burn under cold running water. Do not put grease or butter on it. Cold water helps to take the heat out, but grease or butter will only keep it in.
9. If grease or cooking oil catches fire, throw baking soda or salt at the bottom of the flame to put it out. (Water will *not* put out a grease fire.) Call for help, and try to turn all the stove burners to "off."

HANDLING CHILIES

Fresh chilies have to be handled with care because they contain oils that can burn your eyes or mouth. After working with chilies, be sure not to touch your face until you have washed your hands thoroughly with soap and water. To be extra cautious, wear rubber gloves while fixing chilies. The way you cut the peppers will affect their "hotness." If you take out the seeds, the flavor will be sharp but not fiery. If you leave the seeds in, beware!

METRIC CONVERSION CHART

WHEN YOU KNOW		MULTIPLY BY	TO FIND	
MASS (weight)				
ounces	(oz)	28.0	grams	(g)
pounds	(lb)	0.45	kilograms	(kg)
VOLUME				
teaspoons	(tsp)	5.0	milliliters	(ml)
tablespoons	(Tbsp)	15.0	milliliters	
fluid ounces	(oz)	30.0	milliliters	
cup	(c)	0.24	liters	(l)
pint	(pt)	0.47	liters	
quart	(qt)	0.95	liters	
gallon	(gal)	3.8	liters	
TEMPERATURE				
Fahrenheit	(°F)	5/9 (after	Celsius	(°C)
temperature		subtracting 32)	temperature	

COMMON MEASURES AND THEIR EQUIVALENTS

3 teaspoons = 1 tablespoon

8 tablespoons = ½ cup

2 cups = 1 pint

2 pints = 1 quart

4 quarts = 1 gallon

16 ounces = 1 pound

INDEX
*(recipes indicated by **bold face** type)*

A
aloo mattar, **33**
apple chutney, **43**

B
beat, 15
before you begin, 12-17
beverages, 46
    salty yogurt drink, **47**
    spiced tea, **46**
boil, 15
bread, 44
    deep-fried whole wheat, **45**
    unleavened whole wheat, **44-45**

C
cardamom pods, 13
careful cook, the, 48
carrots with grated coconut, **31**
cayenne pepper, 13
channa dal, **38**
chapatis, **44-45**
chatni, 42
chicken, yogurt, **27**
chickpeas, 12
    curried, **38**
chilies, 13
    handling, 48
chutney, 42
    apple, **43**
    fresh coriander, **42**
cilantro, 13
cinnamon, stick, 13
coconut, 14

flaked, 14
milk, 14
colander, 14
cooking terms, 15
cooking utensils, 14-15
coriander, 13
chutney, fresh, **42**
cumin, 13
curried chickpeas, **38**
curry leaves, 13
curry, pumpkin, **34-35**

D
dal, 37
curried chickpeas, **38**
lentils with garlic and onion, 37
deep-fried stuffed savory pastries, **20-21**
deep-fried whole wheat bread, **45**
dhanya chatni, **42**

E
electric grinder, 14

F
fenugreek, 13
fillet, 15
fish, spicy fried, **28**
fresh coriander chutney, **42**

G
gajar nariyal, **31**
garam masala, 16, **24**
garbanzo beans, 12
garlic, 13
garnish, 15
ginger, 13
green chili, 13

ground lamb kebabs, **25**

H
handling chilies, 48
Hinduism, 8, 9

I
India
food of, 8-9
languages of, 8
people of, 7-8
religions of, 8, 9
Indian meals, 16-17
ingredients, special, 12-14
Islam, 8, 9

K
kabab masala, **25**
kebabs, ground lamb, **25**
kela ka raita, **39**
kheema, **23**
kheera ka raita, **41**
kheera-tamatar raita, **41**
knead, 15

L
lamb kebabs, ground, **25**
lassi, **47**
lentils, 12
split red, 13
with garlic and onion, **37**

M
masala chai, **46**
masoor dal, **37**
meat dishes
deep-fried stuffed savory pastries, **20-21**
ground lamb kebabs, **25**

spiced ground meat, **23**
yogurt chicken, **27**
menu, 18-19
metric conversion chart, 49
muchli masala, **28**
murg dahi, **27**
mustard seed, 13

P
paste, 15
pinay ke liye, **46**
potatoes and peas, **33**
preparing Indian foods, 16
preparing spices, 16
pulao, **29**
pulses (*see dal*), 12
pumpkin curry, **34-35**
puris, **45**

R
raita, 39
yogurt and bananas, **39**
yogurt with cucumber and mint, **41**
yogurt with cucumber and tomato, **41**
rice, spiced, **29**
roast, 15
roti, 44
rub, 15

S
salty yogurt drink, **47**
sambar, **34-35**
samosas, **20-21**
sheb ki chatni, **43**
sieve, 15
simmer, 15

skewer, 15
slotted spoon, 15
spatula, 15
special ingredients, 12-14
spiced
    ground meat, **23**
    rice, **29**
    tea, **46**
spices, 11
    and seasonings, 13
    garam masala, 16, **24**
    preparing, 16
spicy fried fish, **28**
stick cinnamon, 13
T
tea, spiced, **46**
turmeric, 13
U
unleavened whole wheat bread, **44**
utensils, cooking, 14-15
V
vegetarian dishes
    carrots with grated coconut, **31**
    potatoes and peas, **33**
    pumpkin curry, **34-35**
    spiced rice, **29**
W
wok, 15
Y
yogurt
    and bananas, **39**
    chicken, **27**
    drink, salty, **47**
    with cucumber and mint, **41**
    with cucumber and tomato, **41**

ABOUT THE AUTHOR

Vijay Madavan was born and raised in Kamunting, Taiping, Perak, West Malaysia. It was in Malaysia that her grandparents settled after growing up in Kerala, India. Madavan remembers well the Indian influences of both her parents and grandparents, especially in the field of cooking. As a girl, Madavan (along with her two sisters) learned the art of Indian cooking from her mother and still practices it today.

After receiving her B.A. in Business Administration from Stamford College in London, Madavan moved to Minnesota in 1981, where she now lives with her husband, Steve.

The author would like to thank the following people for their help and encouragement: Emily, Adam, Patty and Bob, Sharon, Ethel and Jules, and her many friends around the world, especially Henry.

easy menu
ethnic
cookbooks

Cooking the **AFRICAN** Way
Cooking the **AUSTRALIAN** Way
Cooking the **AUSTRIAN** Way
Cooking the **CARIBBEAN** Way
Cooking the **CHINESE** Way
Cooking the **ENGLISH** Way
Cooking the **FRENCH** Way
Cooking the **GERMAN** Way
Cooking the **GREEK** Way
Cooking the **HUNGARIAN** Way
Cooking the **INDIAN** Way
Cooking the **ISRAELI** Way
Cooking the **ITALIAN** Way
Cooking the **JAPANESE** Way
Cooking the **KOREAN** Way
Cooking the **LEBANESE** Way
Cooking the **MEXICAN** Way
Cooking the **NORWEGIAN** Way
Cooking the **POLISH** Way
Cooking the **RUSSIAN** Way
Cooking the **SOUTH AMERICAN** Way
Cooking the **SPANISH** Way
Cooking the **THAI** Way
Cooking the **VIETNAMESE** Way
DESSERTS Around the World
HOLIDAY Cooking Around the World
How to Cook a **GOOSEBERRY FOOL**
VEGETARIAN Cooking Around the World

Bright yellow turmeric and other spices add color and a special taste to ordinary white-fish fillets. (Recipe on page 28.)